Welcome to
Our State's
Christmas Kitchen

Published by Our State Magazine
Greensboro, North Carolina

Published by Our State Magazine
P.O. Box 4552
Greensboro, N.C. 27404
(800) 948-1409
www.ourstate.com

Printed in the United States by R.R. Donnelley
Cover photography by John Autrey, Emulsion Photography

Our State
NORTH CAROLINA

Library of Congress Cataloging-in-Publication Data

Our state's Christmas kitchen.
    p. cm.
  Includes index.
  ISBN 978-0-9779681-5-2 (alk. paper)
  1. Christmas cookery--North Carolina. I. Our state (Greensboro, N.C.)
  TX739.2.C45O76 2009
  641.5'686--dc22

                    2009016277

Acknowledgments

Although having too many cooks in the kitchen often ruins a recipe, producing a useful and attractive cookbook requires the help of many hands. Primary accolades go to all the folks who contributed the recipes for *Our State's Christmas Kitchen:* our regular contributors, readers from throughout the decades, and members of the *Our State* staff. Without their talent and generosity, our pages would be bare.

Our State magazine is also grateful to food stylist Charlotte Fekete and photographer John Autrey of Emulsion Photography and their assistant, Lacey Suzanne Sombar, for setting up and capturing the enticing images sprinkled throughout the book.

And many thanks to: editor Diane Jakubsen and book designer Katherine Dayton for compiling and designing this volume; to Elizabeth Hudson, Heather Hans, and Mandy Stovall for editorial support; and to production director Cheryl Bissett for guiding the book through production.

CHRISTMAS FUDGE

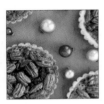

Our State's Christmas Kitchen

As winter's chill begins to take hold, we start
stringing our eaves with lights and draping our
doorways with evergreens. But Christmas doesn't
really stir in our souls until we're rolling up our
sleeves in the kitchen — or, at least, pulling
up a chair to the table.

Welcome to *Our State's Christmas Kitchen*. Here,
we reconnect with traditional treats collected
over 76 years of recipe treasure hunting. You may
recognize some favorites from past issues, like Sweet
Potato Pudding (*November 1999*) and Shrimp-tini
Cocktails (*December 2007*). We've also reached
back to our roots with selections gathered from
our grandmothers' kitchens and assembled in *The
State's Carol Dare Cookbook*, published in 1971. And
because all traditions start somewhere, we're
excited to share some fresh delectables, like Pork
Tenderloin Medallions with Raspberry Sauce
and Pecan-and-Chocolate Tarts.

The aromas, flavors, and textures of North Carolina
cooking transport us to holidays mellowed by
memory and bring our families and friends back to
the table again and again. May the delights you
find in *Our State's Christmas Kitchen* make
your celebrations all the merrier.

CRANBERRY CHRISTMAS PUNCH

Cupola House Wassail

Eggnog

Mulled Cider

Cranberry Christmas Punch

Zesty Feta Cheese Spread

Shrimp-tini Cocktails

CUPOLA HOUSE WASSAIL

1 gallon apple cider

1/2 cup dry lemonade mix
(made with sugar, not artificial sweetener)

2 teaspoons ground cloves

1/2 teaspoon ground allspice

2 sticks cinnamon

1 quart dry white wine

Mix together all ingredients except the wine. Heat in a large pot on the stove. Add the wine, stir to blend, and serve.

Reprinted from Our State, *December 2008*

Cupola House, Edenton

Built in 1758 by Francis Corbin, land agent for the Earl of Granville, this grand Jacobean home was originally a center for British government business and was later home to loyal patriot Dr. Samuel Dickinson. Today, the home, owned by the Cupola House Association, is open for tours and plays host to a Wassail Bowl celebration during Edenton's annual holiday home tour each December.

EGGNOG

4 egg yolks

1 cup plus 2 tablespoons confectioners' sugar

1 1/3 cups apple brandy

2 2/3 cups whipping cream

1 1/3 cups milk

Nutmeg to taste

Beat egg yolks in a mixing bowl until light. Add confectioners' sugar, brandy, whipping cream, and milk one at a time, beating well after each addition. Pour into a punch bowl. Sprinkle with nutmeg.

If desired, an equivalent amount of pasteurized egg substitute may be used to avoid raw eggs. If omitting brandy, egg substitute is recommended.

From Seaboard to Sideboards, *by the Junior League of Wilmington. Reprinted from* Our State, *December 2002*

Notes: _____

_____

_____

_____

_____

MULLED CIDER

6-8 whole cloves

11 teaspoons dried orange peel

2-3 sticks cinnamon

orange slices

lemon spices

1 gallon apple cider

1/2 cup brown sugar

juice of 1 lemon

Tie cloves, orange peel, cinnamon, and orange and lemon slices in cheesecloth bag. Heat all ingredients together, and allow to simmer at least 30 minutes (the longer, the better). Serve hot.

Erica Derr, Greensboro
Reprinted from Our State, *December 2002*

Your Source for Cider

Finding locally made cider shouldn't be too hard in North Carolina, the seventh largest apple-producing state in the nation. And you're in luck if you happen to live near Henderson County, which grows 65 percent of our state's apple crop.

Visit **www.historichendersonville.org/apple_orchards.htm** to learn where you can buy fresh or even pick your own.

CRANBERRY CHRISTMAS PUNCH

2 cups light rum or pineapple juice

1/2 cup sugar

1 12-ounce can frozen orange juice concentrate, thawed and undiluted

1 32-ounce bottle cranberry juice, chilled

1 28-ounce bottle ginger ale, chilled

orange slices

Combine rum, sugar, orange, and cranberry juices. Just before serving, add ginger ale and ice cubes. Garnish with orange slices. Makes 2 1/2 quarts.

Barbara Francisco, Washington
Reprinted from Our State, *December 2002*

Notes: _____

_____

_____

_____

_____

_____

ZESTY FETA CHEESE SPREAD

7 ounces feta cheese
4 tablespoons extra virgin olive oil
1 teaspoon white vinegar
cayenne pepper to taste
1 radish for garnish

Put all ingredients into a food processor, and blend to desired smoothness and consistency. Use a spatula to scoop cheese spread into a serving bowl.

Optional:
To spice it up a little, add roasted red peppers or garlic and herbs to spread.

For garnish:
Clean and trim radish, then use a sharp paring knife to carefully cut the radish in half with a zigzag pattern, like a crown or flower.

Serve room temperature with crackers, pita chips, or toasted white French bread.

Anna Katsoulis, Greenville
Reprinted from Our State, *December 2007*

SHRIMP-TINI COCKTAILS

1 16-ounce jar salsa
1 small ripe avocado, peeled and chopped
1 tablespoon fresh cilantro leaves, chopped
1 tablespoon Texas Pete or other hot sauce
1 tablespoon lime juice
1 pound large shrimp, cooked, peeled, and deveined
1 cup French-fried onions
1 lime, cut into 6 wedges

Combine salsa, avocado, cilantro, hot sauce, and lime juice in a large bowl. Spoon salsa mixture into 6 martini or margarita glasses, filling halfway. Divide shrimp evenly among the glasses, arranging them attractively.

Microwave the French-fried onions on high for 1 minute until hot. Sprinkle over shrimp.

Garnish with lime wedges. Serves 6.

Erica Derr, Greensboro
Reprinted from Our State, *December 2007*

For the freshest shrimp, buy local.

Tar Heel fishermen haul in nearly 5 million pounds of shrimp annually. Brown shrimp, which can grow up to nine inches long, are North Carolina's primary catch, accounting for roughly 66 percent of our state's shrimp landings.

Source: North Carolina Department of Environment and Natural Resources

PORK TENDERLOIN MEDALLIONS
WITH RASPBERRY SAUCE

Pork Tenderloin Medallions with
Raspberry Sauce

Christmas Tree Salad

LeRoy's Holiday Cranberry Sauce

Apricot Chicken with
Parmesan Noodles

Lobster-Stuffed Tenderloin of Beef

Pork Loin Roast

Cooked Goose

Holiday Dressing

Chestnut Dressing

Yorkshire Pudding

Mama Ar's Potato Latkes

Potato Croquettes

Sweet Potato Pudding
in Orange Shells

Holiday Muffins

Maple Sweet Potato Muffins

Broccoli-and-Garden-Pea Casserole

PORK TENDERLOIN MEDALLIONS WITH RASPBERRY SAUCE

2 pounds pork tenderloin, cut crosswise into 1-inch-thick medallions

cayenne pepper to taste

4 tablespoons butter

12 tablespoons raspberry preserves

4 tablespoons red wine vinegar

1 tablespoon horseradish

garlic powder to taste

kiwi fruit, peeled and sliced (optional)

fresh raspberries (optional)

Lightly sprinkle medallions with cayenne pepper. Heat butter in heavy skillet over medium high heat (will need to do two batches). Brown medallions quickly in butter, turning once (3 to 4 minutes per side). Do not overcook. Combine remaining ingredients (except kiwi and fresh raspberries) in saucepan, and simmer for 3 minutes. Serve garnished with sauce and fruits, if desired.

Makes 6 servings

Diane Martin, Our State *Account Supervisor*

CHRISTMAS TREE SALAD

2 small packages lime Jello
1 pint hot water
1 cup cold water
1 cup fruit cocktail syrup
2 1/2 cups fruit cocktail
8 ounces cream cheese
milk

Dissolve Jello in hot water. Add cold water and fruit cocktail syrup. Cool. Then add fruit cocktail. Divide among 8 or 10 cone-shaped paper cups. Set each in a small glass to hold upright. Chill until firm.

After you unmold salad, mix cream cheese with enough milk to soften it so that it will go through the stem end of a decorator. Make circles of cream cheese around the Christmas tree until it's covered. The cream cheese may be colored and flowers and leaves added for further decoration.

Mrs. Raymond Monroe, Laurel Hill, 1951
Reprinted from Carol Dare Cookbook

Notes: _____

_____

_____

_____

LEROY'S HOLIDAY CRANBERRY SALAD

1 cup ground raw cranberries (measure after putting
through food processor)
1/4 cup sugar
1 small package lemon Jello
1/2 cup boiling water
1 cup orange juice
2 teaspoons grated orange rind
1 9-ounce can crushed pineapple
1/2 cup broken pecan meats
1/2 cup chopped celery

Mix sugar and cranberries together, and let stand several
hours. Add Jello to the boiling water, and stir until
dissolved. Add orange juice and stir, then add cranberries
and other ingredients, and pour into mold. Serve on crisp
lettuce, and garnish with mayonnaise.

Nu-Wray Hotel, Burnsville, 1951
Reprinted from Carol Dare Cookbook

Notes: _____

_____

_____

_____

_____

APRICOT CHICKEN WITH PARMESAN NOODLES

2-3 pounds chicken, any kind
1 jar apricot preserves
1 package dry onion soup mix
1 large bottle French dressing

Place the chicken in a baking dish. Mix the remaining ingredients together in a small bowl. Cover the chicken with the sauce. Bake at 350° until done. Serve with Parmesan noodles.

PARMESAN NOODLES

1 package egg noodles
1/2 cup Parmesan cheese
1/4 pound butter
8 ounces cream cheese
1 egg yolk

Cook noodles according to package directions. Combine other ingredients, and stir into warm noodles. Serve warm, and add extra Parmesan cheese as desired.

Lynn Tutterow, Our State *Associate Publisher*

LOBSTER-STUFFED TENDERLOIN OF BEEF

3-4 pounds whole beef tenderloin

2 4-ounce lobster tails

1 tablespoon melted butter

1 1/2 teaspoons lemon juice

6 slices bacon, partially cooked

1/2 cup sliced green onions

1/2 cup butter

1/2 cup dry white wine

1/8 teaspoon garlic powder

Cut tenderloin lengthwise to within 1/2 inch of bottom. Place frozen lobster tails in boiling salted water to cover, and simmer 5 minutes. Remove lobster from shells and cut in half. Place pieces end to end in beef cut. Combine melted butter and lemon juice, and drizzle on lobster. Close beef edges together, and tie with string. Place on rack in roasting pan. Bake at 425° for 30 minutes. Place bacon on top of beef, and roast 5 to 10 minutes. Saute onion in butter in saucepan. Add wine and garlic powder, and heat thoroughly. Spoon wine sauce over sliced roast. Makes 8 servings.

Roast may be prepared in advance; chill until ready to roast.

Diane Martin, Our State *Account Supervisor*

PORK LOIN ROAST

4 pounds pork loin rolled roast
1 12-ounce jar cherry preserves
2 tablespoons light corn syrup
1/4 cup red wine vinegar
1/4 teaspoon salt
1/4 teaspoon ground cinnamon
1/4 teaspoon ground nutmeg
1/4 teaspoon ground cloves
1/4 cup slivered toasted almonds

Rub roast with salt and pepper. Cook at 325° uncovered for 2 to 2 1/2 hours or to internal temperature of 180°. Combine all ingredients, except almonds, in a saucepan. Stir over low heat until boiling. Reduce heat, and simmer for 2 minutes. Glaze roast, and add almonds. Return to oven to roast.

Lynn Tutterow, Our State Associate Publisher

Go hog wild at Nahunta Pork Center in Pikeville, the largest all-pork retail displayer in the eastern United States.

Take your pick from more than 35 different cuts of fresh pork, sausages made from a handed-down family recipe, and salt-cured country hams.

www.nahuntapork.com

COOKED GOOSE

1 goose
salt and pepper to taste
water
1 onion, whole
2-3 tablespoons flour

First, shoot your goose. Then get somebody else to dress him. These are important steps.

Rub with salt and pepper, and put in a boiler with about 3 fingers of water. Add a whole onion. Close lid. Cook on top of stove until tender, adding water if needed. Take up goose. Use flour paste to thicken gravy.

That's all. No baking; no stuffing; no exotic herbs and sauces; no soaking; no marination; no precious secrets; just good goose and good goose gravy.

From Carol Dare Cookbook: *Bill Sharpe, publisher of* The State *from 1951 to 1970, said, "There must be hundreds of complicated formulas for cooking wild fowl. The best goose I ever ate was at the late Ray Adams's Corolla Lodge, and it was cooked by Flora, a Banker girl. She gave me her very uncomplicated recipe."*

HOLIDAY DRESSING *

1/4 cup butter
1/2 cup chopped onion
1/2 cup chopped celery (including leaves)
6 cups small bread cubes
1 egg, beaten
1 1/3 teaspoon poultry seasoning
1 teaspoon salt
dash of pepper
bouillon to moisten

Cook onions and celery in butter. Add remaining ingredients, and mix. Next, add bouillon, just enough to moisten well. Spoon lightly into fowl, or bake in a greased dish separately at 325° for 30 to 40 minutes.

* To make oyster dressing, simply add 1/2 pint of oysters, carefully rinsed, to the above.

Reprinted from Carol Dare Cookbook

Who was Carol Dare?

For 54 years, Carol Dare advised readers of *The State* on topics as varied as cooking, sewing, literature, and helpful home tidbits, all with a Tar Heel twist. The name, however, was actually a pseudonym for several writers: Virginia Abernathy, who launched the column in 1936; Doris Goerch Horton (daughter of *The State* founder Carl Goerch); Sallie Sharpe (publisher Bill Sharpe's wife), and Edie Low.

CHESTNUT DRESSING

1 1/2 pounds chestnuts
1/3 cup butter
1 cup stale bread crumbs
1/2 cup scalded milk
salt and pepper to taste

Remove the shells from the chestnuts, and blanch nuts by pouring boiling water over them. Allow them to stand 5 minutes, until the brown skin can be removed with fingers and a knife.

Cook the nuts in boiling salted water until tender, which will take about half an hour. Mash them fine; add the butter and seasoning, also the crumbs, which have had the scalded milk poured over them. Mix well, and stuff lightly into fowl.

From Carol Dare Cookbook

One of North Carolina's most unique and treasured homes is named for a dwarf chestnut tree.

Jeff and Betsy Penn were so enchanted by the diminutive chinquapins that flourished on their Reidsville plantation in the 1920s that they named their estate Chinqua Penn.

YORKSHIRE PUDDING

1/2 cup all-purpose flour
pinch of salt
1 egg, beaten
1 cup milk

Optional: Add a pinch of mixed herbs and/or onion salt and freshly milled black pepper.

Preheat oven to 400°.

Sift the flour and salt into a mixing bowl. Make a well in the center, and pour in the egg and half of the milk. Beat with a wooden spoon, gradually drawing the flour into the liquid from the sides. When all the flour has been incorporated into the liquid and a thick batter is formed, gradually beat in the remaining milk until the batter is smooth and of a pouring consistency.

Pour the batter into a greased or non-stick baking tin that is approximately 1/2 inch deep. Can be baked as a whole or in individual-sized bun tins. Bake for 40 minutes for a large pudding or 20 minutes for individual ones, or until well risen and golden brown. Serve immediately.

Recommended to accompany beef roast.

Diane Martin, Our State *Account Supervisor*

MAMA AR'S POTATO LATKES

3 large potatoes
1 large onion
1 egg
matzo meal
garlic powder
salt
pepper

Grate potatoes and onion. Drain off water, and blend in egg. Add about 1/4 to 1/2 cup of matzo meal to firm up the mix.

Add seasoning to taste.

Heat a deep frying pan, and add a little vegetable oil. When the pan is very hot and the oil starts to sizzle, add a small ladle of the mix to form small cakes. When the latke is nice and crispy, flip it, and fry the other side. Drain on paper towels. Serve with applesauce and sour cream.

Arlene Gutterman, Our State *Account Supervisor*

Thanks to a predominance of potato growers in our Coastal Plain counties, the versatile vegetable is guaranteed a place on any Southern dinner table.

Celebrate the ubiquitous spud each spring in Elizabeth City, home to the annual North Carolina Potato Festival, where activities include a potato peeling contest, potato sack races, and the crowning of Little Miss Tater Tot.

www.ncpotatofestival.com

POTATO CROQUETTES

2 tablespoons milk
pinch of salt
1/2 teaspoon pepper
2 tablespoons finely chopped green onion
2 egg yolks, beaten
3 tablespoons all-purpose flour
1 tablespoon grated Parmesan cheese
4 cups mashed potatoes
1 egg, beaten
dried bread crumbs
cooking oil, enough to fill pan 1/2-inch deep

Combine milk, salt, pepper, green onion, beaten egg yolks, flour, Parmesan cheese, and mashed potatoes. Chill for about 30 minutes.

Make croquettes using an ice cream scoop, or shape them into balls in your hands. Dip them in the beaten egg, then roll through the bread crumbs. Fry each croquette in hot oil, turning to brown on all sides. Try to leave ample space around each croquette while frying to prevent any crumbling. Makes about 1 dozen croquettes.

Erica Derr, Greensboro
Reprinted from Our State, *November 2007*

SWEET POTATO PUDDING IN ORANGE SHELLS

3 large oranges, cut in halves
3 cups cooked, mashed sweet potato
2 eggs, lightly beaten
1/2 cup dark brown sugar, packed
1/2 teaspoon cinnamon
dash of ground cloves
1/2 stick butter, melted
1 teaspoon vanilla
3/4 cup golden raisins
1/2 cup chopped pecans
fresh orange juice, as needed
6 marshmallows

Scoop pulp from orange halves, and save in a large mixing bowl. Stir in mashed sweet potato, eggs, brown sugar, cinnamon, and cloves, mixing well. Blend in melted butter, vanilla, raisins, and nuts.

Starting with 2 tablespoons orange juice, add only enough juice to make mixture easy to stir, but not soupy. Mound mixture into orange shells. Place in a casserole dish just big enough to hold the shells upright. (A muffin pan with large cups may be even better.)

Bake at 325° for about 30 minutes. Remove from the oven. Place a marshmallow on top of each and return to the oven until melted, about 2 minutes. Serve at once. Makes 6 servings.

Edie Low, Rock Hill, South Carolina
Reprinted from Our State, *November 1999*

HOLIDAY MUFFINS

1 3/4 cups flour

1/2 teaspoon salt

3 teaspoons baking powder

1 teaspoon cinnamon

6 tablespoons sugar or white corn syrup

3/4 cup milk

1 egg

4 tablespoons melted shortening

1 teaspoon vanilla

1/2 cup diced crystallized pineapple

1/2 cup diced dates

1/4 cup broken pecans

Preheat oven to 325°.

Sift flour with salt, baking powder, cinnamon, and sugar or syrup. Add milk, beaten egg, and vanilla, then add melted shortening; stir until all the ingredients are blended but not too smooth. Add pineapple, dates, and nuts. Fill greased muffin tin 2/3 full. Bake for 15 minutes, then sprinkle muffins lightly with sugar. Finish baking 10 more minutes. These are nice served piping hot with afternoon tea.

Mary Vanstory Elzemeyer, Greensboro, 1942
Reprinted from Carol Dare Cookbook

MAPLE SWEET POTATO MUFFINS

1 cup mashed sweet potatoes

1 1/2 cups all-purpose flour

3/4 cup firmly packed brown sugar

2 teaspoons baking powder

1 teaspoon baking soda

3/4 teaspoon ground cinnamon

dash salt

2 large eggs, slightly beaten

3/4 cup salad oil

1/4 cup maple syrup

1/2 cup chopped toasted pecans

1/2 cup currants

Preheat oven to 350°.

In large bowl, combine sweet potatoes, flour, brown sugar, baking powder, baking soda, cinnamon, and salt. Add eggs, oil, and maple syrup; blend well. Stir in pecans and currants. Spoon evenly into greased muffin cups, filling each 3/4 full. Bake for 15 minutes or until muffins spring back when lightly touched. Remove muffins from pan, and serve warm. Makes 1 1/2 dozen muffins.

From the North Carolina Sweet Potato Commission
Reprinted from Our State, *December 2004*

BROCCOLI-AND-GARDEN-PEA CASSEROLE

2 10-ounce packages frozen, chopped broccoli

1 can garden peas, drained

1 can cream of mushroom soup

1 cup mayonnaise

1 teaspoon salt

1/2 teaspoon black pepper

1 cup sharp cheddar cheese, grated

1 medium onion, chopped

2 eggs, beaten

1/2 cup crushed Ritz crackers

Cook broccoli according to package directions. Drain and arrange half of cooked broccoli in a 2-quart casserole dish. Cover with peas.

In a large bowl, mix soup, mayonnaise, salt, pepper, cheese, onion, and eggs. Pour half of the mixture over the broccoli and peas. Add remaining broccoli and top with remaining sauce. Sprinkle with crushed crackers, and bake at 350° for 30 minutes.

Susan Jones, Fuquay-Varina
Mother of Katherine Dayton, Our State *Art Assistant*

PECAN-AND-CHOCOLATE TARTS

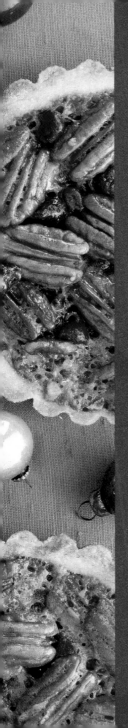

Pecan-and-Chocolate Tarts

Cranberry Coconut Holidainty

Pumpkin Parfait Squares

Holiday Chocolate Cake with
Chocolate Icing

Pumpkin Bread with
Cream Cheese Frosting

Turtle Bars

Breadmaker Moravian
Sugar Cake

PECAN-AND-CHOCOLATE TARTS

1 recipe basic tart dough, chilled

3/4 cup light brown sugar

1/4 cup light corn syrup

1 1/2 tablespoons unsalted butter, melted

2 large eggs

1 teaspoon vanilla extract

1/8 teaspoon salt

1 1/2 cups pecan halves

3/4 cup semi-sweet chocolate chips

Preheat oven to 350°. On a lightly floured board, gently knead and divide tart dough into 4 equal-sized balls. Roll out each ball into a 6-inch round, about 1/8 inch thick, and press into 4 lightly greased 4 1/4-inch fluted tart pans with removable bottoms. Trim edges, and prick base all over with fork. Let shells chill in refrigerator for 15 minutes, and then bake until set and lightly browned, about 15 minutes. Let cool while preparing filling.

In a large bowl, whisk together brown sugar, corn syrup, and melted butter. Whisk in eggs, vanilla, and salt; stir in pecans and chocolate chips. Divide filling between tart shells. Bake for 30 to 35 minutes or until crust is golden brown and filling is bubbly. Let cool slightly before serving.

Charlotte Fekete, Watkinsville, Georgia
Reprinted from Our State, *December 2008*

BASIC TART DOUGH

8 tablespoons unsalted butter, softened

1/2 cup granulated sugar

2 large egg yolks

1 teaspoon water

1/4 teaspoon salt

1 1/3 cups all-purpose flour

In the bowl of an electric mixer fitted with the paddle attachment, beat butter and sugar together until creamy. Add egg yolks, water, and salt; mix to combine. Add flour, and mix until dough is moist and in several medium-sized clumps. Using your hands, form dough into a ball and flatten slightly into a disc. Wrap dough tightly with plastic wrap, and chill until completely firm, about 2 hours. Makes 1 disc, enough for one 9-inch tart or four 4 1/4-inch tarts.

Charlotte Fekete, Watkinsville, Georgia
Reprinted from Our State, *December 2008*

It's no wonder pecan pies are a North Carolina holiday favorite.

Our state produces three to five million pounds of pecans annually, with the highest concentration of pecan orchards, stretching across 2,000 acres, located east of Interstate 95.

Source: North Carolina Pecan Growers Association

CRANBERRY COCONUT HOLIDAINTY

3 cups fresh cranberries
1 1/4 cups water
2 cups sugar
1/2 cup orange juice
1 cup sifted all-purpose flour
1 1/4 teaspoons double-acting baking powder
1/4 teaspoon salt
1/4 cup sugar
1/2 cup coconut, chopped
1 unbeaten egg
1/4 cup butter or margarine, melted and cooled
2 tablespoons orange juice or water

Combine cranberries, water, and sugar in large, wide saucepan or skillet. Bring to a boil, and cook 5 minutes. Remove from heat. Add 1/2 cup orange juice.

Sift together into mixing bowl flour, baking powder, salt, and sugar. Add coconut. Beat egg until light and fluffy; stir in butter and 2 tablespoons orange juice. Add to dry ingredients; mix only until thoroughly moistened.

Heat cranberry mixture again to boiling. Drop dough by tablespoonfuls into simmering cranberries, dipping spoon into cold water each time. Cover tightly; cook 20 minutes over medium heat. Do not remove cover during cooking. Serve warm; top with cranberry sauce or whipped cream. Serves 8.

Reprinted from Carol Dare Cookbook

PUMPKIN PARFAIT SQUARES

1 1/2 cups graham cracker crumbs

1 cup butter, melted

1/4 cup sugar

1/2 cup pecans, finely chopped

1 quart vanilla ice cream

1 1/2 cups cooked or canned mashed pumpkin

1/2 cup brown sugar

1/2 teaspoon salt

1/2 teaspoon cinnamon

1/4 teaspoon ginger

1/8 teaspoon powdered cloves

whipped cream, optional

chopped pecans, optional

Combine crumbs, butter, sugar, and chopped nuts. Press mixture firmly against sides and bottom of 9-inch square pan. Bake in 375° oven for 8 minutes. Cool. Soften ice cream to custard consistency. Mix together pumpkin, brown sugar, salt, cinnamon, ginger, and cloves. Stir pumpkin mixture into ice cream. Pile into cooled crumb crust. Place in freezer until hard. Wrap with foil to store. Remove from freezer 20 minutes before serving. Cut into 3-inch squares. Garnish center of each square with whipped cream and additional chopped nuts, if desired. Yield: 9 squares.

Reprinted from Carol Dare Cookbook

HOLIDAY CHOCOLATE CAKE WITH CHOCOLATE ICING

1 cup butter

2 cups sugar

8 eggs, separated

2 1/2 cups sifted flour

1 teaspoon baking powder

1/4 teaspoon salt

1 teaspoon soda

1 cup buttermilk

4 to 6 ounces chocolate, melted

1 teaspoon vanilla

Preheat oven to 350°.

Cream butter, and beat in sugar. Beat in well-beaten egg yolks. Mix and sift the flour, baking powder, and salt.

Dissolve soda in buttermilk. Add alternately with the dry ingredients to the butter mixture. Mix in melted chocolate, then fold in 6 stiffly beaten egg whites and vanilla.

Turn into 3 buttered and floured layer-cake pans and bake for 30 to 35 minutes (be careful not to overbake as it will become too dry). When cooled, layer cakes and cover with chocolate icing (covering 3-layer cake requires a double-recipe of the icing on page 41.)

CHOCOLATE ICING

2 egg yolks

1 1/2 cups sugar

1/2 cup milk

1 tablespoon butter

dash of salt

4 ounces chocolate

1 teaspoon vanilla

Beat egg yolks until light. Add sugar, and blend well. Add milk, butter, and salt. Melt chocolate in double boiler. Bring the milk mixture to the boiling point, stirring constantly. Cook for a minute or two. Remove from heat. Add the melted chocolate and vanilla. Cool, then beat until of desired consistency.

Cake and icing recipes from Mrs. R.L. McMillan, Raleigh, 1942
Reprinted from Carol Dare Cookbook

Notes: _____

_____

_____

_____

_____

PUMPKIN BREAD WITH CREAM CHEESE FROSTING

1 2/3 cups sugar

6 tablespoons butter

4 eggs

1 16-ounce can pumpkin

2/3 cup water

2/3 cup raisins

1/2 cup chopped nuts

3 1/2 cups all-purpose flour

2 teaspoons baking powder

2 teaspoons cinnamon

cream cheese frosting (optional)

Preheat oven to 350°. Cream sugar and butter. Add eggs one at a time. Stir in pumpkin, water, raisins, and nuts, blending well. Sift together the flour, baking powder, and cinnamon. Stir flour into sugar mixture, blending well. Divide dough between 2 greased loaf pans. Bake for about 1 hour, or until an inserted knife comes out clean. Cool, then frost with cream cheese frosting, if desired.

Susan Rogers
Reprinted from Our State, *November 1997*

CREAM CHEESE FROSTING

8 ounces cream cheese, softened

1/4 cup butter, softened

1 pound confectioners' sugar

1 teaspoon vanilla

Cream together the cream cheese and butter until soft and fluffy. Gradually add sugar, beating well after each addition. Blend in vanilla.

Evelyn Burton
Reprinted from Our State, *November 1994*

National Notice

During the first weekend in October each year, the town of Spring Hope, population 1,400, makes way for more than 40,000 visitors as people pour in for the National Pumpkin Festival. Since 1971, the area chamber of commerce has celebrated this fall favorite with two full days of music, food, crafts, a parade, and contests for the largest pumpkin, best recipe, and most creative decorations.

TURTLE BARS

1/2 cup vegetable shortening
1/4 cup butter
1 1/4 cups brown sugar, packed
2 tablespoons milk
1 teaspoon vanilla
1 egg, lightly beaten
1 3/4 cups all-purpose flour
1/2 teaspoon salt
3/4 teaspoon baking soda
1 1/2 cups semi-sweet chocolate chips
1 14-ounce package caramels
1 tablespoon water

Blend shortening, butter, and sugar until creamy. Blend in milk and vanilla. Beat in egg. Sift together the flour, salt, and baking soda. Stir into creamed mixture only until blended. Stir in chocolate.

Spread 2/3 of dough evenly in a buttered 9 x 13 x 2-inch pan. Combine caramels and water in top of a double boiler. Stir constantly until caramels melt. Spread melted caramel on top of dough in pan, to within 1/2 inch of edge. Spread remaining 1/3 of dough in dollops over top of caramel layer.

Bake at 350° for 25 to 30 minutes, or until golden brown. Be careful not to overbake. Cool completely on a rack. Cut into bars. Makes about 4 dozen 1 x 2-inch bars.

Maggie Peeler, Mountain Grove
Reprinted from Our State, *November 1994*

BREADMAKER MORAVIAN SUGAR CAKE

3/4 cup water
3 tablespoons softened butter
1/4 cup shortening
1 egg, beaten
3/4 cup sugar
1/2 teaspoon salt
2 1/2 cups bread flour
1/2 cup potato flakes
2 teaspoons active dry yeast

Topping:
1/4 cup melted butter
1/2 cup sugar
1/2 cup brown sugar
2 teaspoons cinnamon

Place sugar cake ingredients in order in machine set on dough setting. When done, knead dough on lightly floured surface for 5 minutes. Spread in greased 13 x 9-inch pan, cover, and set aside to rise in a warm area. When doubled in size, poke holes 1 inch apart all over cake with a wooden spoon. Brush surface of cake with melted butter. Mix remaining topping ingredients, and sprinkle over cake, making sure to fill holes.

Bake at 350° for 15 minutes or until golden brown.

Diane Jakubsen, Our State *Senior Editor*

Angel Bars

Archie and Robert's
Holiday Cookies

Christmas Kisses

Cranberry Cookies

Stained-Glass Cookies

Christmas Fudge

ANGEL BARS

1/2 cup butter
1 cup graham cracker crumbs
1/2 cup butterscotch chips
1/2 cup white chocolate chips
1 cup coconut, flaked
1 can sweetened condensed milk
1 cup chopped walnuts

Preheat oven to 325°. Coat bottom of 9 x 9-inch pan with melted butter. Spread graham cracker crumbs evenly over butter, and press into bottom of pan. Sprinkle butterscotch and white chocolate chips evenly over top of the graham cracker crumbs. Sprinkle with flaked coconut. Pour sweetened condensed milk evenly over the coconut, and sprinkle chopped walnuts on top. Bake for 30 minutes. Cool completely before cutting into small squares.

Erica Derr, Greensboro
Reprinted from Our State, *December 2000*

The Angel Doll

Asheboro crime writer Jerry Bledsoe surprised fans in 1996 with *The Angel Doll*, a fictional memoir. The novel about a little boy and the true meaning of Christmas offers an excellent way to satisfy that hunger for more than an edible treat. And for a second helping, follow up with the sequel, *A Gift of Angels*.

ARCHIE AND ROBERT'S HOLIDAY COOKIES

1 cup butter

1 cup light brown sugar

1 cup molasses or honey

3 1/2 cups sifted cake flour

2 1/2 cups sifted all-purpose flour

2 teaspoons salt

1 tablespoon pumpkin pie spice

1/4 teaspoon ground cloves

2 teaspoons soda

4 tablespoons hot water

Preheat oven to 325°. Cream butter, add sugar and molasses or honey, and beat until well blended. Mix and sift pre-sifted cake and all-purpose flours, salt, and spice. (Add more or less spice according to own taste.) Add dry ingredients to the butter mixture.

Dissolve soda in hot water, and mix into the dough. Chill overnight in refrigerator. Roll a small piece of the dough at a time on a floured surface. If chilled thoroughly, it can be rolled almost paper thin.

Shape with floured Christmas cutters into wreaths, Santas, lambs, stars, Christmas trees, angels, etc. Bake for 10 minutes. Cool on wire rack. Decorate as desired.

Mrs. R.L. McMillan, Raleigh, 1942
Reprinted from Carol Dare Cookbook

CHRISTMAS KISSES

2 egg whites
1 cup powdered sugar
1 cup chopped nut meats (or 1/2 cup nuts and 1/2 cup coconut)
1 cup chopped dates (or mixed candied fruit)
1 teaspoon lemon, vanilla, or rum flavoring

Preheat oven to 275°. Beat egg whites until stiff; add sugar, and fold in thoroughly. Add remaining ingredients, and drop by spoonfuls on cookie sheet coated with cooking spray. Bake for 20 minutes.

From Favorite Recipes of the Lower Cape Fear
Reprinted from Carol Dare Cookbook

Looking for calorie-free Christmas Kisses?

Cultivate a recipe for acquiring a holiday kiss by growing your own mistletoe. L.A. Jackson, *Our State*'s longtime gardening columnist, offers these steps to starting a mistletoe plant:
1. Find a low limb of a deciduous tree (oak, poplar, maple) that is at least as big around as your thumb and that gets plenty of sunlight.
2. Make a small, shallow, angled cut into the bark and squeeze a seed out of a mistletoe berry into the cut. The sticky juice will hold the seed in place.
3. Repeat about six times on a three- to four-inch portion of the limb, and wait for germination. Plant this year, and your homegrown mistletoe will be ready for next Christmas.

CRANBERRY COOKIES

1/2 cup butter, softened
1/4 cup solid shortening
1 1/4 cups light brown sugar, packed
1 egg
1/3 cup milk (skim is fine)
1 1/2 teaspoons vanilla
1 teaspoon grated orange peel
1 cup all-purpose flour
1/2 teaspoon baking soda
1/2 teaspoon salt
3 cups uncooked quick oats
1 cup dried cranberries
1 cup coarsely chopped walnuts

Preheat oven to 375°. Beat butter, shortening, and sugar together until light and fluffy.

Stir in egg, milk, vanilla, and orange peel, then beat at medium mixer speed until well blended. Sift flour with baking soda and salt, then blend with oats. Add to creamed mixture, stirring just until blended. Mixture will be stiff. Stir in cranberries and nuts. Place a tablespoonful of dough at a time on a greased cookie sheet, each 2 inches apart.

Bake 12 to 14 minutes, or until golden. Cool a minute or so on cookie sheet, then remove to a rack to finish cooling. Makes roughly 4 dozen cookies.

Susan Masson, Asheville
Reprinted from Our State, *December 1993*

STAINED-GLASS COOKIES

1/2 cup margarine

1/2 cup sugar

1/2 cup honey

1 egg, beaten

1 teaspoon vanilla extract

3 cups flour

1 teaspoon baking powder

1/2 teaspoon baking soda

1/2 teaspoon salt

9 ounces LifeSavers candies, approximately

Preheat oven to 350°. Cream margarine, sugar, honey, egg, and vanilla in a mixing bowl. Mix in flour, baking powder, baking soda, and salt. Cover tightly and refrigerate for 2 hours. Turn dough onto a lightly floured surface and roll out to 1/4-inch thickness. With a set of nesting cookie cutters, first use the largest size cutter to make the cookies, then use the smallest of that shape in the center of the cookies to make the "windows." Place the cut-out shapes on baking sheets lined with foil. Next, crush each color of candies separately between layers of wax paper. Spoon crushed candy into the "windows" of cookies. Bake for 6-8 minutes, or until candy is melted and cookies are lightly brown. Cool completely before removing from foil.

Erica Derr, Greensboro
Reprinted from Our State, *December 2000*

CHRISTMAS FUDGE

2 cups sugar

1/2 teaspoon salt

1/2 stick butter

1 5-ounce can evaporated milk

1 12-ounce package semi-sweet chocolate chips

1 7.5 ounce Symphony chocolate bar with almonds
and toffee bits

1 7-ounce jar marshmallow creme

2 teaspoons vanilla extract

2 cups coarsely chopped walnuts or pecans

Heavily butter a 9 x 13-inch baking pan and set aside. Place
the sugar, salt, butter, and evaporated milk in a large, heavy
saucepan. Bring to a boil over medium-high heat, stirring
constantly. When the mixture comes to a boil, reduce
heat to medium. Boil gently for 8 to 9 minutes, stirring
frequently to make sure the bottom does not scorch. Stir in
the chocolate chips, chocolate bar, and marshmallow creme
until the mixture is well blended. Stir in the vanilla extract
and nuts. Pour the mixture into the prepared pan. Cool at
room temperature for several hours or until set. Cut into
1-inch squares. Store in an airtight container for up to 2
weeks, if they aren't consumed long before that.

Erica Derr, Greensboro
Reprinted Our State, *from December 2000*

GINGERBREAD

Gingerbread

Cranberry Vinegar

Garlic Vinegar

Cheese Ball

Chocolate Chip Cheese Ball

Cocktail Pecans

Chocolate Taffy

Butter Pecan Pound Cake

Jeff's Bourbon Balls

GINGERBREAD

2 eggs

3/4 cup brown sugar

3/4 cup molasses

3/4 cup melted shortening

2 1/2 cups flour

2 teaspoons baking soda

1/2 teaspoon baking powder

1 1/2 teaspoons cinnamon

1/3 teaspoon cloves

1/3 teaspoon nutmeg

2 teaspoons ginger

1 cup boiling water

Preheat oven 350°. Grease a 9 x 13-inch pan (no smaller).
Mix together eggs and sugar, and molasses and shortening.
In a separate bowl, sift together flour, baking soda, baking
powder, cinnamon, cloves, nutmeg, and ginger. Combine
the two mixtures, then slowly stir in the boiling water.
Bake 30 to 35 minutes (be careful not to overbake as it will
become too dry).

From Carol Dare Cookbook

CRANBERRY VINEGAR

1 cup white vinegar
1 cup fresh cranberries

Combine vinegar and cranberries in a small pot. Bring to a boil, reduce heat, and boil gently until cranberries pop. Turn mixture into a glass or plastic container. Cover and let stand at room temperature for 3 days.

Place 2 coffee filters in a strainer. Set strainer in a bowl. Pour cranberry mixture into filters, letting vinegar strain into the bowl. Discard cranberries. Pour vinegar into a sterilized decorative glass bottle. Store in refrigerator up to 3 weeks. Makes about 1 cup.

GARLIC VINEGAR

1 pint cider vinegar
6 cloves garlic, peeled, halved

Bring vinegar to a rolling boil. Pour into a jar, add garlic, and let stand at room temperature overnight. Remove garlic, strain vinegar into a sterilized decorative bottle. Keeps about 1 month. Makes 1 pint.

Both recipes on this page from Edie Low, Rock Hill, South Carolina
Reprinted from Our State, *December 1997*

CHEESE BALL

24 ounces cream cheese, softened

8 ounces sour cream

8 ounces cheddar cheese, grated

2 tablespoons mayonnaise

1 teaspoon garlic salt

1 teaspoon Worchestershire sauce

1 cup chopped pecans

Mix all ingredients thoroughly in a mixer. Shape into 3 or 4 balls and chill. Roll in chopped nuts. Can freeze.

Lynn Tutterow, Our State *Associate Publisher*

Notes: _____

_____

_____

_____

_____

_____

_____

_____

CHOCOLATE CHIP CHEESE BALL

8 ounces cream cheese, softened
1 stick butter, softened
3 tablespoons brown sugar
3/4 cup powdered sugar
1 teaspoon vanilla
1 cup mini chocolate chips
chopped pecans

Mix cream cheese and butter. Add sugars and vanilla. Fold in chocolate chips. Mold into ball, and roll in pecans. Refrigerate overnight. Serve with graham cracker sticks.

Lynn Tutterow, Our State *Associate Publisher*

With 26 licensed cheese makers in the state, according to the N.C. Department of Agriculture, we're tops among the Southern states in cheese production.

Enjoy the "fruits" of our cheese makers' labors with a visit to Ashe County Cheese Company in West Jefferson, the oldest cheese manufacturer in North Carolina. In production since 1930, Ashe County Cheese Co. relies on daily fresh milk deliveries to produce its signature Original Mountain Cheddar. For another taste of artisanal cheese, head to Yellow Branch Farm and Pottery in Robbinsville, where owners Karen Mickler and Bruce DeGroot milk their own herd of Jersey cows to produce small quantities of high-quality, handcrafted cheese.

106 East Main Street, West Jefferson • (800) 445-1378
www.ashecountycheese.com

136 Yellow Branch Circle, Robbinsville • (828) 479-6710
www.yellowbranch.com

COCKTAIL PECANS

1 pound pecan halves
1/4 cup butter
1 tablespoon Worcestershire sauce
Tabasco sauce to taste
salt to taste

Place nuts in a bowl. Melt butter in a small pan. Stir in Worcestershire sauce and 2 to 4 drops of Tabasco. Blend well, and sample. Add a few more drops of Tabasco only if you like a hot, tangy taste. Pour sauce over pecans, stirring to coat well. Spread nuts on a baking sheet. Sprinkle lightly with salt. Bake at 300° for 20 minutes, stirring every 5 minutes. Spread on several layers of paper towels on a rack to cool. Store in airtight containers. Makes about 2 cups.

Edie Low, Rock Hill, South Carolina
Reprinted from Our State, *December 1997*

Notes: _____

_____

_____

_____

_____

_____

CHOCOLATE TAFFY

1 cup brown sugar

1/3 cup corn syrup

2/3 cup water

1 cup molasses

1/4 teaspoon salt

2 tablespoons butter

4 ounces chocolate, melted

1 tablespoon vanilla

Mix first six ingredients, and cook slowly, stirring constantly, until the mixture begins to boil. Cook to soft crack stage (270°–290°). Pour into buttered pan, and pour chocolate over it. As edges cool, fold toward the center. Add vanilla, and fold until cool enough to pull. Pull and fold until mixture is no longer shiny, and then cut into pieces with buttered kitchen scissors. Wrap the pieces in wax paper, and store in a closed tin for best results.

From Out of Our League, by the Junior League of Greensboro
Reprinted from Our State, February 2004

Taffy of Torpedo Junction

Re-released in 1996, Nell Wise Wechter's 1957 novel about 13-year-old Taffy Tillis's discovery of a Nazi spy ring on the Outer Banks continues to captivate young readers with adventures based on the startling reality that German U-boats preyed on and sank 60 American ships off the North Carolina coast during World War II.

BUTTER PECAN POUND CAKE

1/4 cup powdered sugar

1/4 cup chopped pecans

1 box butter pecan cake mix

4 eggs

3/4 cup oil

1 cup milk

1 container coconut-pecan icing

Dust tube or Bundt pan with powdered sugar after greasing. Sprinkle chopped pecans on bottom. Combine cake mix, eggs, oil, and milk until smooth. Stir in icing. Pour over pecans. Bake at 325° for 55-60 minutes or until brown. Cool 20 minutes before turning on a cake plate.

Jennifer Francis, Our State *Office Manager*

Good taste by the pound

Pound cake gets its name from the original recipe, believed to have traveled to the New World from Great Britain: one pound of sugar, one pound of butter, one pound of eggs, and one pound of flour, beat together thoroughly for one hour. Or, save yourself the trouble, and contact The Pound Cake Company in Benson for its blue-ribbon pound cakes in a variety of sizes, which can be delivered to your door.

310 South Lee Street, Benson, N.C. 27504
(919) 894-8448 • www.thebestcake.com

JEFF'S BOURBON BALLS

1 6-ounce package chocolate bits

1/2 cup sugar

3 tablespoons light corn syrup

1/2 cup bourbon

1 1/2 cups vanilla wafers, finely crushed

1 cup walnuts or pecans, finely chopped

powdered sugar, sifted

Melt chocolate in top of double boiler. Remove from heat. Stir in sugar and corn syrup. Add bourbon, and blend well. Combine vanilla wafer crumbs and nuts in a large bowl. Add chocolate mixture, and blend well. Form into one-inch balls. Roll in powdered sugar. Place in airtight container for three to 10 days, then enjoy. Makes 40 balls. Wrap individually, and arrange in decorative tins or gift bags for holiday giving.

From Modern Recipes from Historic Wilmington
by the Lower Cape Fear Historical Society, Wilmington
Reprinted from Our State, *December 2005*

Notes: _____

_____

_____

_____

_____

_____

Index